PUSH

I WILL STAY FOCUSED. I WILL DO THE WORK.
I WILL SUCCEED.

A 52- WEEKLY JOURNAL

YOLANDA MARSHALL NICKERSON

Published by Glimpse of Glory Christian Book Publishing
ISBN: 978-1-7364667-0-4

Printed in the United States of America

Unless otherwise identified, all Scripture quotations in this publication are from the NIV, NLT and GNT Bible.

Ladies, I am very excited about the level of success that you will experience. I want to be one of the people who will someday say, "She was determined to succeed, and she did." If you are focused on accomplishing your goals and seeing your dreams manifest, you will begin to scratch each goal off your list one by one by putting in the necessary work and never entertaining the thought of quitting. Don't allow anything or anyone distract you. Make sure you connect with people who want to see you flourish and succeed in whatever you aspire to do. "Surround yourself with only people who are going to lift you Higher." -Oprah Winfrey.

You can use the journal sections of this book to write down what you would like to accomplish each week of this year. As you write down your weekly goal(s), you can write a personal affirmation and a prayer for that week, too. "The prayer of a good person has a powerful effect." -James 5:16-GNT.

Stay focused. Do the work. You will succeed. PUSH.

Yolanda Marshall Nickerson

WRITE DOWN YOUR GOALS FOR THIS YEAR

"For I can do everything through Christ, who gives me strength." -Philippians 4:13-NLT

1. ______________________________
2. ______________________________
3. ______________________________
4. ______________________________
5. ______________________________
6. ______________________________
7. ______________________________
8. ______________________________
9. ______________________________
10. ______________________________
11. ______________________________
12. ______________________________
13. ______________________________

14. ______________________________________

15. ______________________________________

16. ______________________________________

17. ______________________________________

18. ______________________________________

19. ______________________________________

20. ______________________________________

WEEK 1

"For I can do everything through Christ, who gives me strength." -Philippians 4:13-NLT

What would you like to accomplish this week and how do you plan to achieve it?

Write your personal affirmation.

Communicate with God through prayer. Write your own pray.

Reminder: Make sure you connect with people who want to see you flourish and succeed in whatever you aspire to do.

WEEK 2

"For I can do everything through Christ, who gives me strength." -Philippians 4:13-NLT

What would you like to accomplish this week and how do you plan to achieve it?

Write your personal affirmation.

Communicate with God through prayer. Write your own pray.

Reminder: Make sure you connect with people who want to see you flourish and succeed in whatever you aspire to do.

WEEK 3

"For I can do everything through Christ, who gives me strength." -Philippians 4:13-NLT

What would you like to accomplish this week and how do you plan to achieve it?

Write your personal affirmation.

____

____

____

____

____

____

Communicate with God through prayer. Write your own pray.

____

____

____

____

____

____

____

____

____

____

____

____

____

***Reminder**:* Make sure you connect with people who want to see you flourish and succeed in whatever you aspire to do.

WEEK 4

"For I can do everything through Christ, who gives me strength." -Philippians 4:13-NLT

What would you like to accomplish this week and how do you plan to achieve it?

Write your personal affirmation.

____

____

____

____

____

____

Communicate with God through prayer. Write your own pray.

____

____

____

____

____

____

____

____

____

____

____

____

____

Reminder: Make sure you connect with people who want to see you flourish and succeed in whatever you aspire to do.

WEEK 5

"For I can do everything through Christ, who gives me strength." -Philippians 4:13-NLT

What would you like to accomplish this week and how do you plan to achieve it?

Write your personal affirmation.

Communicate with God through prayer. Write your own pray.

Reminder: Make sure you connect with people who want to see you flourish and succeed in whatever you aspire to do.

WEEK 6

"For I can do everything through Christ, who gives me strength." -Philippians 4:13-NLT

What would you like to accomplish this week and how do you plan to achieve it?

Write your personal affirmation.

____

____

____

____

____

____

Communicate with God through prayer. Write your own pray.

____

____

____

____

____

____

____

____

____

____

____

____

____

Reminder*:* Make sure you connect with people who want to see you flourish and succeed in whatever you aspire to do.

WEEK 7

"For I can do everything through Christ, who gives me strength." -Philippians 4:13-NLT

What would you like to accomplish this week and how do you plan to achieve it?

Write your personal affirmation.

____

____

____

____

____

____

Communicate with God through prayer. Write your own pray.

____

____

____

____

____

____

____

____

____

____

____

____

____

Reminder: Make sure you connect with people who want to see you flourish and succeed in whatever you aspire to do.

WEEK 8

"For I can do everything through Christ, who gives me strength." -Philippians 4:13-NLT

What would you like to accomplish this week and how do you plan to achieve it?

Write your personal affirmation.

____

____

____

____

____

____

Communicate with God through prayer. Write your own pray.

____

____

____

____

____

____

____

____

____

____

____

____

____

Reminder: Make sure you connect with people who want to see you flourish and succeed in whatever you aspire to do.

WEEK 9

"For I can do everything through Christ, who gives me strength." -Philippians 4:13-NLT

What would you like to accomplish this week and how do you plan to achieve it?

Write your personal affirmation.

____

____

____

____

____

____

Communicate with God through prayer. Write your own pray.

____

____

____

____

____

____

____

____

____

____

____

____

____

***Reminder**:* Make sure you connect with people who want to see you flourish and succeed in whatever you aspire to do.

WEEK 10

"For I can do everything through Christ, who gives me strength." -Philippians 4:13-NLT

What would you like to accomplish this week and how do you plan to achieve it?

Write your personal affirmation.

____

____

____

____

____

____

Communicate with God through prayer. Write your own pray.

____

____

____

____

____

____

____

____

____

____

____

____

____

Reminder: Make sure you connect with people who want to see you flourish and succeed in whatever you aspire to do.

WEEK 11

"For I can do everything through Christ, who gives me strength." -Philippians 4:13-NLT

What would you like to accomplish this week and how do you plan to achieve it?

Write your personal affirmation.

____

____

____

____

____

____

Communicate with God through prayer. Write your own pray.

____

____

____

____

____

____

____

____

____

____

____

____

____

Reminder: Make sure you connect with people who want to see you flourish and succeed in whatever you aspire to do.

WEEK 12

"For I can do everything through Christ, who gives me strength." -Philippians 4:13-NLT

What would you like to accomplish this week and how do you plan to achieve it?

Write your personal affirmation.

____

____

____

____

____

____

Communicate with God through prayer. Write your own pray.

____

____

____

____

____

____

____

____

____

____

____

____

____

***Reminder**:* Make sure you connect with people who want to see you flourish and succeed in whatever you aspire to do.

WEEK 13

"For I can do everything through Christ, who gives me strength." -Philippians 4:13-NLT

What would you like to accomplish this week and how do you plan to achieve it?

Write your personal affirmation.

____

____

____

____

____

____

Communicate with God through prayer. Write your own pray.

____

____

____

____

____

____

____

____

____

____

____

____

____

***Reminder**:* Make sure you connect with people who want to see you flourish and succeed in whatever you aspire to do.

WEEK 14

"For I can do everything through Christ, who gives me strength." -Philippians 4:13-NLT

What would you like to accomplish this week and how do you plan to achieve it?

Write your personal affirmation.

Communicate with God through prayer. Write your own pray.

Reminder: Make sure you connect with people who want to see you flourish and succeed in whatever you aspire to do.

WEEK 15

"For I can do everything through Christ, who gives me strength." -Philippians 4:13-NLT

What would you like to accomplish this week and how do you plan to achieve it?

Write your personal affirmation.

Communicate with God through prayer. Write your own pray.

Reminder: Make sure you connect with people who want to see you flourish and succeed in whatever you aspire to do.

WEEK 16

"For I can do everything through Christ, who gives me strength." -Philippians 4:13-NLT

What would you like to accomplish this week and how do you plan to achieve it?

Write your personal affirmation.

Communicate with God through prayer. Write your own pray.

Reminder: Make sure you connect with people who want to see you flourish and succeed in whatever you aspire to do.

WEEK 17

"For I can do everything through Christ, who gives me strength." -Philippians 4:13-NLT

What would you like to accomplish this week and how do you plan to achieve it?

Write your personal affirmation.

____

____

____

____

____

____

Communicate with God through prayer. Write your own pray.

____

____

____

____

____

____

____

____

____

____

____

____

____

***Reminder**:* Make sure you connect with people who want to see you flourish and succeed in whatever you aspire to do.

WEEK 18

"For I can do everything through Christ, who gives me strength." -Philippians 4:13-NLT

What would you like to accomplish this week and how do you plan to achieve it?

Write your personal affirmation.

____

Communicate with God through prayer. Write your own pray.

Reminder: Make sure you connect with people who want to see you flourish and succeed in whatever you aspire to do.

WEEK 19

"For I can do everything through Christ, who gives me strength." -Philippians 4:13-NLT

What would you like to accomplish this week and how do you plan to achieve it?

Write your personal affirmation.

____

Communicate with God through prayer. Write your own pray.

***Reminder**:* Make sure you connect with people who want to see you flourish and succeed in whatever you aspire to do.

WEEK 20

"For I can do everything through Christ, who gives me strength." -Philippians 4:13-NLT

What would you like to accomplish this week and how do you plan to achieve it?

Write your personal affirmation.

Communicate with God through prayer. Write your own pray.

Reminder: Make sure you connect with people who want to see you flourish and succeed in whatever you aspire to do.

WEEK 21

"For I can do everything through Christ, who gives me strength." -Philippians 4:13-NLT

What would you like to accomplish this week and how do you plan to achieve it?

Write your personal affirmation.

____

____

____

____

____

____

Communicate with God through prayer. Write your own pray.

____

____

____

____

____

____

____

____

____

____

____

____

____

Reminder: Make sure you connect with people who want to see you flourish and succeed in whatever you aspire to do.

WEEK 22

"For I can do everything through Christ, who gives me strength." -Philippians 4:13-NLT

What would you like to accomplish this week and how do you plan to achieve it?

Write your personal affirmation.

Communicate with God through prayer. Write your own pray.

Reminder: Make sure you connect with people who want to see you flourish and succeed in whatever you aspire to do.

WEEK 23

"For I can do everything through Christ, who gives me strength." -Philippians 4:13-NLT

What would you like to accomplish this week and how do you plan to achieve it?

Write your personal affirmation.

Communicate with God through prayer. Write your own pray.

Reminder: Make sure you connect with people who want to see you flourish and succeed in whatever you aspire to do.

WEEK 24

"For I can do everything through Christ, who gives me strength." -Philippians 4:13-NLT

What would you like to accomplish this week and how do you plan to achieve it?

Write your personal affirmation.

____

____

____

____

____

____

Communicate with God through prayer. Write your own pray.

____

____

____

____

____

____

____

____

____

____

____

____

____

Reminder: Make sure you connect with people who want to see you flourish and succeed in whatever you aspire to do.

WEEK 25

"For I can do everything through Christ, who gives me strength." -Philippians 4:13-NLT

What would you like to accomplish this week and how do you plan to achieve it?

Write your personal affirmation.

Communicate with God through prayer. Write your own pray.

Reminder: Make sure you connect with people who want to see you flourish and succeed in whatever you aspire to do.

WEEK 26

"For I can do everything through Christ, who gives me strength." -Philippians 4:13-NLT

What would you like to accomplish this week and how do you plan to achieve it?

Write your personal affirmation.

____

____

____

____

____

____

Communicate with God through prayer. Write your own pray.

____

____

____

____

____

____

____

____

____

____

____

____

____

Reminder: Make sure you connect with people who want to see you flourish and succeed in whatever you aspire to do.

WEEK 27

"For I can do everything through Christ, who gives me strength." -Philippians 4:13-NLT

What would you like to accomplish this week and how do you plan to achieve it?

Write your personal affirmation.

Communicate with God through prayer. Write your own pray.

Reminder: Make sure you connect with people who want to see you flourish and succeed in whatever you aspire to do.

WEEK 28

"For I can do everything through Christ, who gives me strength." -Philippians 4:13-NLT

What would you like to accomplish this week and how do you plan to achieve it?

Write your personal affirmation.

____

____

____

____

____

____

Communicate with God through prayer. Write your own pray.

____

____

____

____

____

____

____

____

____

____

____

____

____

***Reminder**:* Make sure you connect with people who want to see you flourish and succeed in whatever you aspire to do.

WEEK 29

"For I can do everything through Christ, who gives me strength." -Philippians 4:13-NLT

What would you like to accomplish this week and how do you plan to achieve it?

Write your personal affirmation.

____

____

____

____

____

____

Communicate with God through prayer. Write your own pray.

____

____

____

____

____

____

____

____

____

____

____

____

____

Reminder: Make sure you connect with people who want to see you flourish and succeed in whatever you aspire to do.

WEEK 30

"For I can do everything through Christ, who gives me strength." -Philippians 4:13-NLT

What would you like to accomplish this week and how do you plan to achieve it?

Write your personal affirmation.

____

Communicate with God through prayer. Write your own pray.

____

Reminder: Make sure you connect with people who want to see you flourish and succeed in whatever you aspire to do.

WEEK 31

"For I can do everything through Christ, who gives me strength." -Philippians 4:13-NLT

What would you like to accomplish this week and how do you plan to achieve it?

Write your personal affirmation.

Communicate with God through prayer. Write your own pray.

Reminder: Make sure you connect with people who want to see you flourish and succeed in whatever you aspire to do.

WEEK 32

"For I can do everything through Christ, who gives me strength." -Philippians 4:13-NLT

What would you like to accomplish this week and how do you plan to achieve it?

Write your personal affirmation.

____

____

____

____

____

____

Communicate with God through prayer. Write your own pray.

____

____

____

____

____

____

____

____

____

____

____

____

____

Reminder: Make sure you connect with people who want to see you flourish and succeed in whatever you aspire to do.

WEEK 33

"For I can do everything through Christ, who gives me strength." -Philippians 4:13-NLT

What would you like to accomplish this week and how do you plan to achieve it?

Write your personal affirmation.

____

____

____

____

____

____

Communicate with God through prayer. Write your own pray.

____

____

____

____

____

____

____

____

____

____

____

____

____

Reminder: Make sure you connect with people who want to see you flourish and succeed in whatever you aspire to do.

WEEK 34

"For I can do everything through Christ, who gives me strength." -Philippians 4:13-NLT

What would you like to accomplish this week and how do you plan to achieve it?

Write your personal affirmation.

Communicate with God through prayer. Write your own pray.

Reminder: Make sure you connect with people who want to see you flourish and succeed in whatever you aspire to do.

WEEK 35

"For I can do everything through Christ, who gives me strength." -Philippians 4:13-NLT

What would you like to accomplish this week and how do you plan to achieve it?

Write your personal affirmation.

Communicate with God through prayer. Write your own pray.

Reminder: Make sure you connect with people who want to see you flourish and succeed in whatever you aspire to do.

WEEK 36

"For I can do everything through Christ, who gives me strength." -Philippians 4:13-NLT

What would you like to accomplish this week and how do you plan to achieve it?

Write your personal affirmation.

____
____
____
____
____
____

Communicate with God through prayer. Write your own pray.

____
____
____
____
____
____
____
____
____
____
____
____
____

Reminder: Make sure you connect with people who want to see you flourish and succeed in whatever you aspire to do.

WEEK 37

"For I can do everything through Christ, who gives me strength." -Philippians 4:13-NLT

What would you like to accomplish this week and how do you plan to achieve it?

Write your personal affirmation.

____
____
____
____
____
____

Communicate with God through prayer. Write your own pray.

____
____
____
____
____
____
____
____
____
____
____
____
____

Reminder: Make sure you connect with people who want to see you flourish and succeed in whatever you aspire to do.

WEEK 38

"For I can do everything through Christ, who gives me strength." -Philippians 4:13-NLT

What would you like to accomplish this week and how do you plan to achieve it?

Write your personal affirmation.

Communicate with God through prayer. Write your own pray.

Reminder: Make sure you connect with people who want to see you flourish and succeed in whatever you aspire to do.

WEEK 39

"For I can do everything through Christ, who gives me strength." -Philippians 4:13-NLT

What would you like to accomplish this week and how do you plan to achieve it?

Write your personal affirmation.

____

____

____

____

____

____

Communicate with God through prayer. Write your own pray.

____

____

____

____

____

____

____

____

____

____

____

____

____

Reminder: Make sure you connect with people who want to see you flourish and succeed in whatever you aspire to do.

WEEK 40

"For I can do everything through Christ, who gives me strength." -Philippians 4:13-NLT

What would you like to accomplish this week and how do you plan to achieve it?

Write your personal affirmation.

____
____
____
____
____
____

Communicate with God through prayer. Write your own pray.

____
____
____
____
____
____
____
____
____
____
____
____
____

***Reminder**:* Make sure you connect with people who want to see you flourish and succeed in whatever you aspire to do.

WEEK 41

"For I can do everything through Christ, who gives me strength." -Philippians 4:13-NLT

What would you like to accomplish this week and how do you plan to achieve it?

Write your personal affirmation.

____

____

____

____

____

____

Communicate with God through prayer. Write your own pray.

____

____

____

____

____

____

____

____

____

____

____

____

____

Reminder: Make sure you connect with people who want to see you flourish and succeed in whatever you aspire to do.

WEEK 42

"For I can do everything through Christ, who gives me strength." -Philippians 4:13-NLT

What would you like to accomplish this week and how do you plan to achieve it?

Write your personal affirmation.

Communicate with God through prayer. Write your own pray.

Reminder: Make sure you connect with people who want to see you flourish and succeed in whatever you aspire to do.

WEEK 43

"For I can do everything through Christ, who gives me strength." -Philippians 4:13-NLT

What would you like to accomplish this week and how do you plan to achieve it?

Write your personal affirmation.

____

____

____

____

____

____

Communicate with God through prayer. Write your own pray.

____

____

____

____

____

____

____

____

____

____

____

____

____

Reminder: Make sure you connect with people who want to see you flourish and succeed in whatever you aspire to do.

WEEK 44

"For I can do everything through Christ, who gives me strength." -Philippians 4:13-NLT

What would you like to accomplish this week and how do you plan to achieve it?

Write your personal affirmation.

____
____
____
____
____
____

Communicate with God through prayer. Write your own pray.

____
____
____
____
____
____
____
____
____
____
____
____
____

Reminder: Make sure you connect with people who want to see you flourish and succeed in whatever you aspire to do.

WEEK 45

"For I can do everything through Christ, who gives me strength." -Philippians 4:13-NLT

What would you like to accomplish this week and how do you plan to achieve it?

Write your personal affirmation.

____
____
____
____
____
____

Communicate with God through prayer. Write your own pray.

____
____
____
____
____
____
____
____
____
____
____
____
____

Reminder: Make sure you connect with people who want to see you flourish and succeed in whatever you aspire to do.

WEEK 46

"For I can do everything through Christ, who gives me strength." -Philippians 4:13-NLT

What would you like to accomplish this week and how do you plan to achieve it?

Write your personal affirmation.

____

____

____

____

____

____

Communicate with God through prayer. Write your own pray.

____

____

____

____

____

____

____

____

____

____

____

____

____

Reminder: Make sure you connect with people who want to see you flourish and succeed in whatever you aspire to do.

WEEK 47

"For I can do everything through Christ, who gives me strength." -Philippians 4:13-NLT

What would you like to accomplish this week and how do you plan to achieve it?

Write your personal affirmation.

Communicate with God through prayer. Write your own pray.

Reminder: Make sure you connect with people who want to see you flourish and succeed in whatever you aspire to do.

WEEK 48

"For I can do everything through Christ, who gives me strength." -Philippians 4:13-NLT

What would you like to accomplish this week and how do you plan to achieve it?

Write your personal affirmation.

____

____

____

____

____

____

Communicate with God through prayer. Write your own pray.

____

____

____

____

____

____

____

____

____

____

____

____

____

Reminder: Make sure you connect with people who want to see you flourish and succeed in whatever you aspire to do.

WEEK 49

"For I can do everything through Christ, who gives me strength." -Philippians 4:13-NLT

What would you like to accomplish this week and how do you plan to achieve it?

Write your personal affirmation.

Communicate with God through prayer. Write your own pray.

Reminder: Make sure you connect with people who want to see you flourish and succeed in whatever you aspire to do.

WEEK 50

"For I can do everything through Christ, who gives me strength." -Philippians 4:13-NLT

What would you like to accomplish this week and how do you plan to achieve it?

Write your personal affirmation.

____

____

____

____

____

____

Communicate with God through prayer. Write your own pray.

____

____

____

____

____

____

____

____

____

____

____

____

____

Reminder: Make sure you connect with people who want to see you flourish and succeed in whatever you aspire to do.

WEEK 51

"For I can do everything through Christ, who gives me strength." -Philippians 4:13-NLT

What would you like to accomplish this week and how do you plan to achieve it?

Write your personal affirmation.

Communicate with God through prayer. Write your own pray.

Reminder: Make sure you connect with people who want to see you flourish and succeed in whatever you aspire to do.

WEEK 52

"For I can do everything through Christ, who gives me strength." -Philippians 4:13-NLT

What would you like to accomplish this week and how do you plan to achieve it?

Write your personal affirmation.

____

____

____

____

____

____

Communicate with God through prayer. Write your own pray.

____

____

____

____

____

____

____

____

____

____

____

____

____

Reminder: Make sure you connect with people who want to see you flourish and succeed in whatever you aspire to do.

www.ingramcontent.com/pod-product-compliance
Lightning Source LLC
LaVergne TN
LVHW020647100826
845148LV00012B/2367
* 9 7 8 1 7 3 6 4 6 6 7 0 4 *